GETTING A JOB IN
LAW ENFORCEMENT, SECURITY, AND CORRECTIONS

MARY-LANE KAMBERG

ROSEN
PUBLISHING®

NEW YORK

In memory of Roy Kamberg,
Reserve Patrolman, Overland Park, Kansas

Published in 2014 by The Rosen Publishing Group, Inc.
29 East 21st Street, New York, NY 10010

Library of Congress Cataloging-in-Publication Data

Kamberg, Mary-Lane, 1948–.
Getting a job in law enforcement, security, and corrections/by Mary-Lane Kamberg.—1st ed.—New York: Rosen, c2014
        p. cm.—(Job basics: getting the job you need)
Includes bibliographical references and index.
ISBN 978-1-4488-9605-9
1. Law enforcement—Vocational guidance—Juvenile literature.
2. Corrections—Vocational guidance—United States—Juvenile literature. I. Title.
HV7922 K36 2014
363.2'02373

Manufactured in the United States of America

CPSIA Compliance Information: Batch #S13YA: For further information, contact Rosen Publishing, New York, New York, at 1-800-237-9932.

CONTENTS

INTRODUCTION

A police officer chases down a bank robber on foot, rescues a kidnap victim, and solves a cold case murder...all before lunch. A corrections officer uses brains and brawn to stop a prison riot. A security guard thwarts a burglary ring in a warehouse, rounding up six suspects all by himself.

These are examples of a typical day for police officers, corrections officers, and security guards on television or in the movies, not in real life.

Jobs like these are rewarding and challenging. And sometimes they are exciting. They can also be dangerous, demanding, and frustrating.

A typical day as a police officer starts with a shift meeting or roll call. The supervising officer shares information and makes assignments. The next step is to check out the squad car for any damage or mechanical problems. During routine patrol, the officer watches for suspicious activity. The dispatcher sends officers on a variety of calls. The officer may be sent to take a stolen bicycle report, check on someone's welfare, or, yes, occasionally respond to an alarm at a local bank. A police officer deals with many different people from different cultures and backgrounds. He or she must protect and serve them all.

On a typical day, a corrections officer must be ready for anything. A calm, quiet morning can turn into a noisy

Scenes in television shows like *Hawaii Five-0* and movies like *The Dark Knight Rises (above)* often make police officers' jobs seem more exciting and eventful than real-life law enforcement careers.

disturbance, sometimes without warning. Each day the officer meets with the entire shift staff. This meeting is known as the "read off." Supervisors assign where each will work. This area of responsibility is known as the officer's post. Most posts are for housing units. Others include the places new inmates are admitted or released. Officers learn to treat their charges with respect, authority, and patience.

A security officer's typical day varies depending on the employer and type of work. Some work at a desk in a building lobby. They may check for identification or inspect packages coming into the area. Others patrol buildings, inside and out. Still others monitor closed-circuit televisions at casinos or corporations. These jobs may sometimes be exciting or even hazardous. However, most of the time, the goal is prevention of harm to persons, buildings, and personal or company property. A security officer may be asked to give directions, administer first aid, or give advice about security risks. He or she is the first barrier against workplace violence.

To land a job in any of these criminal justice fields, applicants must know the required education, physical fitness, and special training necessary and how to get them. They must be able to find openings and know how to apply for jobs. Such skills include writing a résumé and cover letter and preparing for a job interview. Once they land a position, they need to know how to succeed in the field by adding to skills and knowledge and taking promotion exams. Let's take a look at how to get hired in these fields.

Choosing a Career

D o you have what it takes to be a police officer? Or work in security? Or keep order in a jail?

You might choose a criminal justice career in law enforcement, security, or corrections. Requirements for these jobs vary. For one thing, state laws differ. So do the needs of the agencies that hire people for these jobs.

Where do you look for such jobs? And what do you do to land one? First take a look at some of the choices.

Is Law Enforcement for You?

Police officers have dangerous, high-stress jobs. They meet criminals and crime victims—sometimes in life-threatening situations. They write traffic tickets and accident reports. Police officers must stay alert at all times. They might walk a beat. Or operate a patrol car. Or motorcycle. Or helicopter. And they record everything in official reports. Often, they testify in court. Their jobs put demands on the body and mind.

Police officers usually work eight-hour shifts five days a week. The shifts rotate. That includes days, evenings, and the middle of the night. It also includes weekends and holidays. All twenty-four hours of the day.

One task assigned to police officers is traffic accident investigation. The required reports help insurance companies settle disputes for damages. Sometimes the officers appear in court to describe what they saw.

Benefits vary. Police officers wear uniforms. They usually get a uniform allowance. (Public and private detectives wear civilian clothes.) Benefits usually include medical and dental insurance, as well as a retirement plan. Some places offer early retirement choices.

As their careers move forward, some police officers become detectives to investigate crimes. They work for individuals, law firms, or private companies. They collect evidence and talk to witnesses and suspects. Some become private detectives. They may check someone's background or look for a missing person. They gather facts about financial matters or personal issues.

Minority Hiring

The first police officers in the United States were white males. In 1892, the city of Brooklyn, New York, hired the first African American police officer. In the early 1970s, fewer than 1 percent of police officers were women, according to Police-Officer-Pages.com.

In 1972, the U.S. Supreme Court ruled that the 1964 Civil Rights Act applied to cities. Police departments had to hire without regard to race or gender. Since then the number of women and minorities in police work has grown. According to Police-Officer-Pages.com, 9 percent of police officers in the late 1990s were women. In 2011, that number had grown to 17 percent, according to the *Statistical Abstract of the United States*. And in 2006, the U.S. Department of Justice Statistics said minorities made up 24 percent of all police officers (that had increased from 15 percent in 1987).

Job Requirements

Job requirements for law enforcement vary by state. However, for all police departments, candidates need a high school diploma or they must pass the General Equivalency Degree (GED) test. They must be U.S. citizens, at least twenty-one years of age, and have a driver's license. They

Job applicants in law enforcement fields must often pass a polygraph exam. The test cannot guarantee someone is telling the truth, but it does measure physical reactions that some people experience when they lie.

must be in good health and fitness with good vision and hearing. And their weight must be healthy for their height.

They must pass a background check with no felony convictions. They must qualify to carry a gun according to state law. They must take a polygraph test, drug test, and psychological exam. A polygraph is sometimes called a lie detector. It's a machine that measures changes in heartbeat, blood pressure, and respiration. Physical reactions like these may show that a person is lying. Some police departments make officers live in the city, county, or state where they work.

Employers also look for personal skills. Officers deal with

TAKE A GOOD LOOK AT YOURSELF

Before choosing a career, rate yourself in seven areas. This self-exam will help you decide which jobs best suit you. In conducting the review, be honest. If you're unsure about some traits, ask a friend or family member to discuss them with you. Write answers to the following questions. Putting everything on paper helps focus the effort.

1. What kind of personality do you have?
2. What values are important to you?
3. How much money do you need to make?
4. What are your long-term goals?
5. Make a list of skills you have.
6. Which skills do you like best?
7. Which skills would you like to gain or improve?

Use the answers to see how well you're fit for different jobs. If you want a job you're not yet ready for, acquire those skills. Compare possible careers in terms of your likes, skills, and interests.

many types of people. Police officers need to be good leaders. They often work in teams, so they must work well with others and follow orders.

Law enforcement jobs at the state and federal levels pay more than those in towns and cities. But they are harder to get. They have similar requirements. However, these jobs usually go to applicants with some college credits, bachelor's degrees, or police or military experience. These jobs include state troopers, or highway patrol officers, public transportation police, deputy sheriffs, and fish and game wardens. Agencies such as the Federal Bureau of Investigation (FBI), U.S. Drug Enforcement Administration (DEA), U.S. Secret Service, Federal Air Marshals, and the U.S. Border Patrol require either a bachelor's degree or work experience.

Job opportunities in law enforcement are likely to grow. According to the U.S. Bureau of Labor statistics, the number of jobs in law enforcement is expected to grow 7 percent between 2010 and 2020. For the latest information on pay for police officers and other careers, visit the Web site for the *Occupational Outlook Handbook* from the U.S. Department of Labor's Bureau of Labor Statistics.

Jobs in Security Services

Private companies and individuals want to be safe. And they want to protect their property. Security work varies with the type of job. Security officers work in banks, armored cars, casinos, museums, and office buildings. They also work in bus depots, airports, and railroad stations. They spend their time walking through buildings and around the grounds. Or they sit in a guardhouse or a building lobby.

They might:

More than half of the nation's security officers work for private companies. A store security guard may watch for shoplifting. He or she may also advise the store owner about ways to prevent theft.

- Screen employees and visitors
- Inspect vehicles and deliveries
- Monitor alarms and closed-circuit TV cameras
- Hold suspects
- Talk to witnesses to crimes
- Write daily reports

The work schedule varies. Security staff usually work shifts to cover the job twenty-four hours a day, seven days per week. That includes holidays and weekends. Shifts may be eight hours long for full-time employees. Some security workers do it only part time.

The field of security includes many types of jobs. The U.S. Department of Labor says 53 percent of security jobs were in private security services in 2012. Another 9 percent were in government agencies. Six percent worked on school campuses. Five percent worked for hotels or food service companies. And 4 percent worked in hospitals. Some work as bodyguards. Others install locks or alarm systems.

What It Takes

Security guards must be at least eighteen years of age. Armed guards must be twenty-one. They need a high school diploma or GED. Some jobs require a driver's license. Candidates must be strong and physically fit. They may also have to pass a drug test. Security guards must observe and communicate well. They must make good decisions. Many employers require some post-secondary courses in criminal justice. Some employers check fingerprints and criminal records. Employers also look for honesty.

In most states security guards must be licensed. In some areas they need other training or certifications. Few security guards carry guns. If they do, they need a gun license and additional training. Some security officers become special police officers. They can make arrests. Jobs in security are likely to grow. According to the U.S. Bureau of Labor statistics, opportunities are expected to rise 19 percent between 2010 and 2020.

Corrections

Jails, prisons, and juvenile halls need workers to keep order and enforce rules.

Corrections officers supervise inmates and report conduct. The officers look for drugs and other items inmates are not allowed to have. They may help give advice to inmates. Or they may inspect conditions to be sure they meet proper standards.

Corrections workers must be U.S. citizens or permanently live in the United States. Age requirements range between eighteen and twenty-one years of age. Applicants need a high school diploma or GED. Some jobs require more education after high school. Job seekers need good writing skills. Some employers require some college credits. However, law enforcement or military experience can sometimes substitute for education. A background check must show no felony convictions.

Corrections officers also need to be able to use good judgment to solve problems. The workers may need to stop arguments. So they need good communication and negotiation skills. An officer must control his or her emotions.

Applicants must be strong enough to physically move or restrain inmates.

Corrections officers work for city, state, or federal governments. Or they may find jobs with private companies. Some government agencies hire private firms to staff their facilities. Most officers work eight-hour shifts. The shifts rotate to cover twenty-four hours per day, seven days per week. That includes holidays and weekends. They may have to work paid overtime. Some employers provide uniforms or a clothing allowance. And some offer retirement benefits. The U.S. Department of Labor expects the number of jobs to rise 5 percent between 2010 and 2020.

Meeting Minimums and More

Job seekers need to meet the minimum requirements for any job. In the criminal justice fields, these fall into three general areas: education, physical fitness, and special skills.

First, the applicant must finish high school. A general education is important. But some high school classes are especially helpful. Police officers, security guards, and corrections officers write lots of reports. Those reports are legal documents. Writing must be clear with good grammar and spelling. Classes in composition, creative writing, and journalism help improve writing skills.

A police or corrections officer must be able to speak with authority. He or she must use clear speech when appearing as a witness in a court of law. Speech classes teach public speaking and communication skills. Psychology classes help students prepare for careers where they deal with all types of people.

Math classes teach the basics needed to make drawings and measure distances for car accident reports. Math is important for the use of a firearm or investigating the path of a bullet at a crime scene. Math skills also help in reading a map, which is important in police and security work.

Especially useful is the ability to read a topographical map. This type of map shows the positions and heights above sea level of lakes, rivers, forests, roads, and buildings. One place to

Speech and writing classes teach skills that police officers need. The reports they write are legal documents. And oral communication skills are important in the courtroom.

gain experience in map reading is through orienteering. Orienteering is using a map and compass to find one's way across an unknown area. The Boy Scouts of America and Girl Scouts of the USA are two places to find this kind of program.

Job seekers with no high school diploma must pass the GED test. This exam covers reading, writing, social studies, science, and mathematics. To pass, one needs the skills taught in four years of high school, so it's best to take a class to get ready for it. Reference librarians, high school counselors, and community college officials have information about such classes and where to take the test. Opportunities are also listed online.

SAMPLE QUESTIONS FROM POLICE WRITTEN EXAMS

Written police exams vary by agency. They often test grammar, reading, and math skills. Here are some sample questions:

1. [Rewrite the following sentence:] The suspects untied they're shoes.

2. [Which word is closest to the same meaning as the underlined word?] At the funeral, the murder victim was <u>eulogized</u> by his friends.

    a. praised   b. rescued

    c. delighted   d. forgotten

3. Which of the following choices are NOT in ascending order?

    a. 1, 3, 5   b. 9, 17, 39

    c. -2, -4, -6   d. -85, -75, -65

    e. none of the above

4. Joey has $252.13 in his checking account. He writes checks for $65.89, $120.25, and $72.13. What is the remaining balance in his account?

    a. -$61.40   b. $6.14

    c. -$6.14   d. $32.03

5. After a hit-and-run accident, several witnesses described the fleeing car. Which of the following is most likely to be right?

    a. white Toyota Camry with a car seat in back and a Kansas license plate

    b. white Nissan Maxima with a car seat in back and a Kansas license plate

    c. white Toyota Camry, with clothes hanging in back and a Kansas license plate

    d. beige Toyota Camry with a car seat in back and a Missouri license plate

6. A police officer is off duty. He sees two men having a fistfight. What should he do?
   a. nothing, he's off duty   b. break up the fight
   c. identify himself as a police officer and tell them to stop fighting
   d. call an ambulance if needed after the fight ends

7. An officer's patrol area has seen recent thefts of big-screen TVs. Which of the following observations during her routine patrol should she care most about?
   a. a couple reading an ad for big screen TVs
   b. a teenager riding a bike through the neighborhood at night
   c. two men in a van circling the block
   d. two men unloading a boxed TV from a store van

Answers: 1. The suspects untied their shoes.; 2. a; 3. c; 4. c; 5. a; 6. c; 7. c

Getting Fit

Security workers and police and corrections officers must stay fit. Many jobs require a physical test before hiring. A typical test includes the ability to do a specific number of push-ups, sit-ups, pull-ups, and bench presses. It may also include running 1.5 miles (2.4 km) in less than eight to ten minutes.

High school physical education classes are good places to learn how to get in shape. So are school and club sports teams. Fitness includes strength, endurance, and flexibility. Strength comes from weight-bearing exercise. This may include walking, running, weight lifting, and such exercises as pull-ups, sit-ups, and push-ups.

Careers in criminal justice require physical fitness. Jogging is one way to get in shape. A balanced plan includes whole-body training in strength, fitness, and flexibility.

Endurance means the ability to do an activity for a long period of time. Walking, running, bike riding, and swimming are good ways to build endurance. Flexibility comes from stretching exercises. Again, a fitness professional is the best place to start. City or county parks and recreation departments offer a wide variety of sports and fitness classes. Ask a librarian for books on the subject.

Before starting a fitness program, see a doctor. It's also a good idea to check with a coach or physical education teacher. Ask for help making a training plan. Work toward balanced, whole-body fitness.

Special Skills

Special skills in areas outside criminal justice can help you get the job you want. Were you raised in a bilingual home? You have an advantage. Agencies often look for officers who speak a language in addition to English. The need is especially high for speakers of Spanish, Portuguese, Arabic, Italian, Chinese, and Korean. Look for language classes in high schools, community colleges, or online. Other courses may be available in the community. Do an Internet search for the language you want and the name of your city.

Other helpful skills include first aid and cardiopulmonary resuscitation (CPR). Look for classes at hospitals or through such organizations as the American Heart Association. These skills are important in careers as first responders. So is the ability to drive safely. Private companies and some high schools offer driver's education and defensive driving classes. Finally, knowing firearm safety adds another important skill. Cities, state wildlife departments, parks and recreation agencies, and private companies offer classes.

COMMUNITY COLLEGE CREDIT CLASSES

Many community colleges offer classes toward degrees in criminal justice. Many employers like applicants who have taken some of them, even if the candidate has not completed a degree. Here are some examples of classes frequently offered by community colleges:

- Police operations
- Crime prevention
- Police interrogation
- Juvenile delinquency
- Retail security
- Community-based corrections
- Introduction to terrorism
- Criminal law

Computer and technology skills are important in most twenty-first-century jobs. Work in criminal justice is no exception. The more computer experience you have, the better. Even if you don't know the particular programs the employer uses, the new ones will be easier to learn.

Some organizations offer training for criminal justice jobs. Many are open to those who have not yet taken a job in the field. For example, some police academies are open to non-officers. So are security classes through the International Security Conference and other associations. And such corrections organizations as the American Correctional Association offer conferences for members, including student members.

Real-life Experience

Jobs outside criminal justice also help. For example, public contact jobs like work in a retail store or fast-food restaurant are good practice for dealing with people. So are jobs where communication is important. Office work requires good verbal and written skills through telephone, e-mail, letters, and business reports. Volunteer work also develops some of the same useful traits as paid work.

Experience counts. And some police departments, high schools, and community colleges offer programs for young people interested in criminal justice careers. These internship or work/study programs may include classes as well as office work in the field. In one such program, students tie in classroom work with supervised, real-life situations. Just being around a working environment adds important skills and insights.

Preparing for a Written Test

Part of applying for many criminal justice jobs is passing a written test. Most law enforcement and many corrections agencies require exams. Some security jobs may also ask for one. The tests measure such areas as judgment, problem solving, vocabulary, spelling, grammar, memorization, mathematics, and reading.

There is no single "national" test. Some law enforcement agencies use exams from such companies as Stanard and Associates. Others use tests from such state-based organizations as Peace Officer Standards and Training. Still others write their own tests.

Most criminal justice jobs require applicants to pass a written test. These tests vary from agency to agency. Before taking such an exam, practice with sample questions online.

The types of questions vary. Combinations of true/false, essay, fill-in-the-blank, and multiple-choice questions are common. Some tests include reading sections followed by questions about them. Others ask candidates about situations shown in videos. You can find sample tests with an easy Internet search. Ask the employer if the test is a civil service test. Or, if not, which type it is. Ask where you can find sample tests. The New York State Department of Civil Service, for example, posts an online guide to its entry-level police officer exam. Practice with some samples before taking an employment test.

Finding Job Openings

You're ready to go. But where are the jobs? The first step is to be flexible. Be open to all kinds of opportunities. Don't hold out for one dream job. You might get a job where you can learn and gain experience on the way to the dream job. And don't limit yourself to one place. You may have to move to another city or state to get the job you want.

Study the market. Use online searches to find employers in the field. Are there parts of the state or metro area that are growing? Those are places that will need more police officers. Growth areas are also places to look for all types of security jobs. Is a new prison being built—or expanded—nearby? It will need corrections officers.

Where Are the Job Listings?

City, county, state, and federal Web sites list job openings and qualifications. Other online resources can help, too. Craigslist, for example, lists criminal justice jobs under both "governments" and "security." A Web site called Police Locator lists police departments by state and city. It links to their Web sites and job postings.

You can also use such Internet searches as "security jobs in (your city)," "corrections jobs in (your state,)" or "law

Search the Internet for criminal justice job openings in both your home area and out-of-state. Many agencies post ads for recruits on Web sites or in ads in online magazines.

enforcement jobs in (your area)." Other key words for Internet searches include:

- Police
- Security
- Law enforcement
- Public safety
- Officer
- City (or state) employees
- Prisons
- Jails
- Guards

Many professional magazines run employment ads. Ask a librarian to help you find them. The library may subscribe to some. Or you may find online editions. *American Police Beat*, for example, is an online magazine that lists job openings. The Oklahoma Department of Corrections publishes *Inside Corrections*. Many issues list current job opportunities in that state. And *Security Magazine* has a "Help Wanted" section. And don't forget the local newspaper's online or hard-copy want ads.

Another place to look is criminal justice organizations. The American Correctional Association, for example, has a job bank for members. So does ASIS International (formerly known as the American Society for Industrial Security). A job bank is part of a Web site that lets employers post job openings. It includes requirements for each job. Some include the ability to apply online.

Community bulletin boards (both online and in stores and libraries) often list jobs. Job fairs, recruitment drives, and career days at high schools and in the community are additional resources.

The Hidden Job Market

Governments must advertise job openings. But not all employers do. Some find workers through word of mouth and the recommendations of current employees. These unpublished jobs are known as the hidden job market. The hidden job market also includes openings that someone knows about but that have not yet been posted.

JOB SEARCH TIPS

Successful job seekers share some common practices. Here are some of their tips:

1. Spread the word. Tell everyone who will listen that you're looking for a job. Include the type of job you want.
2. Make a separate cover letter and résumé for each position. Tailor them to the specific job and hiring agency.
3. Proofread everything. Careless typing, bad grammar, and poor spelling doom a letter, e-mail, or résumé.
4. Learn as much as possible about the employer, not just the job.
5. Delete party photos and any other questionable pictures from your social media pages.
6. Act like a pro. Dress for the job you want. Change a "cute" e-mail address to a serious one. Be sure your voice mail message sounds businesslike. Forget show tunes, "funny" voices, and sound effects.
7. Remember manners. Thank everyone who helps in the job search, especially all hiring managers—even if you don't get the job.

The best way to find these jobs is to network. Networking means using friends and other contacts to learn information or share services. Build a network of people you know—and people who know the people you know. They can help you prepare for a job. And they can let you know when they hear about new opportunities.

For example, a law enforcement network might include patrol officers, school resource officers, and Drug Abuse Resistance Education (D.A.R.E.) officers. It could also include state and federal agents—or people you meet at a high school career day or at job fairs.

Building a Network

To build a network, begin by knowing yourself. What are your goals? How do your education and experiences add to your ability to do the job you want? You need to be able to communicate your traits, skills, and long-term goals. You also need to show an employer how they make you a good candidate. In addition, do some homework. Develop a body of information about the type of work you want and the types of employers who have those kinds of jobs.

The next step is to make a list of possible contacts. Who do you want to talk to? What kind of information do you hope to learn? Do you know anyone who works in your field of interest? Do any of your friends or relatives know anyone in the profession you aspire to? Start there.

The more people you ask, the more people you'll find. Ask former teachers. If you've been employed, put your present and past bosses on the list. You might be surprised to know who their connections are. And look for local

Tell everyone you know that you're looking for a certain type of job. Ask for help building a list of contacts who can help you with advice or job opening information.

members of professional organizations who might offer to help. Once you start building your network, ask your contacts to introduce you to others in their fields.

Making Contact

Before you reach out to the people on your list, write a one-minute speech. This is sometimes called an "elevator speech." It's what you would say to a network contact if you could talk only during an elevator ride. Writing the speech will help you focus your thoughts and keep them brief. Sum up your talents

EXAMPLE OF AN ELEVATOR SPEECH

Can you tell someone about the job you want and your skills for it in the time it takes to ride an elevator? An elevator speech lasts about one minute. Here's an example of an elevator speech you can use over the phone or in a letter or e-mail.:

Hello, Mr. Rohrback. My name is Philip Clayton. I hope to find a job as a security officer. I have many traits that are useful in the field. I have good observation skills, I love doing research, and I'm comfortable with today's technology. My communication skills are good. I worked on my school newspaper and won awards for my writing. I can also speak Spanish fluently. My grandmother came from Mexico, and I was raised in a bilingual home.

I'm calling you because I need more information. I hope you'll be willing to meet with me for about twenty minutes. I'd like to learn the best way to present myself to employers, and I would appreciate your comments. May I make an appointment to talk with you about starting my career?

and goals. Write the speech. Practice it. Revise it. Practice some more. Memorize it so that it comes easily and sounds natural.

Make your first contacts with those who are closest to you on your contact list. You'll be less nervous talking to friends, neighbors, and relatives. They will be eager to help you. And you'll gain good practice as well as information. Connect in person. Or use snail mail, e-mail, or such professional social media as LinkedIn. Avoid more casual media. Your contact will take you more seriously if your message is not competing with others' vacation pictures and party shots.

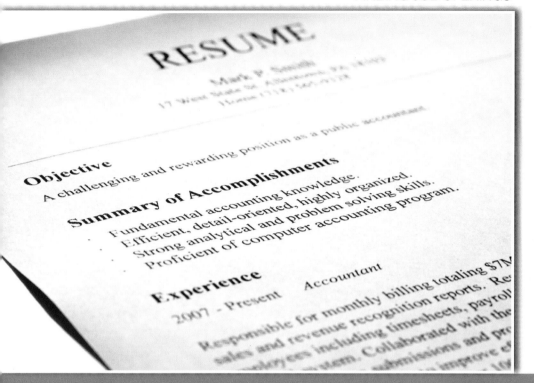

A résumé lists skills, experience, and interests. It is an important part of an employment package that also includes a cover letter and list of references. Tailor a specific package to a specific job.

Prepare for the Meeting

List questions you'd like to ask. This keeps you on track. And it shows that you respect the contact's time. Some typical questions include:

- How did you get into this field?
- What are the best and worst parts of the job?
- What are the best skills I can bring to the job?
- What tips do you have for someone just starting out in the field?
- What are entry-level salaries in this city?

- Do you know anyone else I can contact?
- Do you know of any jobs in the field?

Your contact may have questions for you. Think about what he or she may want to know. Be ready to show your knowledge of the field. Be able to discuss your short-term and long-term goals. And plan to talk about your qualifications and your plans for further education or training.

At the end of the agreed time limit, thank the contact and leave. Be sure the contact has your phone number and e-mail address. He or she may not be able to help you find a job right away, but be sure you can be easily reached if something comes along. Follow up your meeting with a handwritten thank-you note. From time to time during your job search (and later), drop a note or e-mail to stay in touch. And be sure to let the contact know when you are hired. Your contact may help in the future if you seek a promotion or a new job.

Looking Good on Paper

Job applicants need an easy way to show how well they fit employers' needs. An employment package serves that need. It includes a résumé and cover letter. It also has copies of documents and a list of references.

To start, gather all the information you'll need. Include the physical addresses, e-mail addresses, and phone numbers and supervisors' names for past jobs or volunteer work. Make lists of activities and interests. And make copies of such documents as a high school diploma, first-aid card, and certificate from a workshop or other post-high school education.

Preparing a Résumé

A résumé is a first impression on paper. It lists a candidate's skills, experience, and interests. A good résumé highlights the traits most important for the job. One size does not fit all. It's a good idea to make different résumés for different jobs.

Start with your name and contact information. If your name is somewhat common, include a middle name or initial. Instead of Ann Nelson, for example, use Ann L. Nelson or Ann Louise Nelson. If you use a nickname, add it in quotation marks: Edward "Eddie" Jones. However, avoid such odd nicknames as "Fats," "Shorty," or "Killer." Save them for social occasions, not the workplace.

Include home and e-mail addresses and all phone numbers where employers can reach you. (Be sure to leave out a current work phone if you can't take calls from future employers there.) Change your voice mail message to sound professional. Avoid flip phrases, music, and sound effects. Create a separate e-mail account just for the job search. Make the username professional. Avoid cute or off-color phrases. An employer may get a bad impression from such usernames as "sneakypete," "coptobe," or "jailer."

After the name and contact information, add a brief sentence about your career goals. Here's an example:

Objective: To begin a career in private security as an assistant to a private investigator.

What to Include

Divide the rest of the résumé into sections. Under each heading, put the most recent information first. Typical headings include education, training, and employment. Put the strongest section first. For instance, start with "training" if you have little related work experience but have completed a cadet program or internship. Training also includes classes you've taken for other jobs. Perhaps your employer sent you to a diversity training class or to one in CPR. Put the training section first. Add the employment section later.

Some résumés have a section on activities and interests. Use it only if you have a job-related passion. Have you been in a cross-cultural or interfaith group? That shows that you can work well with different kinds of people. Put it down. If

Be sure your résumé paints an accurate picture of your skills, experience, and interests. But leave out hobbies that have no connection with job requirements.

you belong to a martial arts or masters swimming club, add it. These activities emphasize an interest in fitness. But if you like fly fishing or knitting, omit the heading.

Some information does not belong on a résumé. Leave out age, marital status, and family. Omit ethnic background and religious or political beliefs. Ignore salary information—both at previous jobs and what you'd like to make in the future. Leave out your references, too. They belong on a separate sheet. Give them to the employer only when asked. Finally, leave out reasons for leaving past jobs. They open up areas you may not want to discuss in an interview. However, if your reasons for moving on show improved skills and new responsibilities, you might want to include them.

Keep the résumé to one page. Be sure that everything on it is true. Employers in some fields may not check the information, but those in criminal justice will. Print in black ink on white or ivory paper. Criminal justice employers tend to be conservative when it comes to business. Avoid other colors. And leave out graphics. Use a font like Times New Roman with a 10-point to 12-point type size. Don't use all caps, italics, or boldface. Single-space. Check grammar and spelling. And proofread! Twice.

Write a Cover Letter

Never send a résumé alone in an envelope. Be sure it goes to the hiring supervisor by adding a cover letter. A cover letter is just that. It "covers" a résumé. A cover letter is a business letter addressed to a specific person at a specific agency or department. (Avoid the urge to run off dozens of copies of a

SAMPLE COVER LETTER

234 South First Street
Someplace, MO 12345-6789

Day: (555) 456-7890
Evening: (555) 123-4567
Mobile: (555) 765-4321
lawson@xxx.com

March 3, 20—

Mr. Fred Ladewig
Chief of Police
Any Town Police Department
234 North Second Street
Any Town, FL 12345-6789

Dear Chief Ladewig,

I would like to apply for the patrol officer opening advertised in *American Police Beat*. My grandfather was a detective with the Chicago Police Department. I've always wanted to follow in his footsteps.

I grew up in Nearby Town, Florida, and am familiar with the directions to most schools, government buildings, and businesses in Any Town. My teachers have always commented on my hard work and ability to learn new things. I have volunteered as a referee for Midnight Baseball, which aims to curb gang violence.

May I schedule an interview? Thank you for your consideration.

Sincerely,

Jeff Lawson

form letter to save time.) You can design a letterhead. Or simply type the letter. Put the date, your contact information, and the hiring person's name and address. Add a greeting: "Dear Mr. Nelson."

A cover letter has three parts. The first tells why you are sending the résumé. It tells the specific job applied for and why you want the job. If you want to work at the specific agency, say so. And say why. If one of your network contacts referred you, say that. ("Frank Brichet at Pleasant Valley Juvenile Detention Center told me you are looking for a corrections officer.") If you're replying to an advertised position, tell where you saw the ad.

The second paragraph says something about you. In about three sentences, tell your most important traits for the job. Do you have strong verbal skills? Are you good with time management? Have you always wanted to be a police officer? Why? Keep it brief. Leave out information that's already in the résumé.

The third part asks for an interview. (That is the purpose of the résumé in the first place.) You want to get a chance to talk to the hiring person. Keep the cover letter to one page. Again, check grammar and spelling and proofread. Remember to sign the letter in ink between the closing ("Sincerely" or "Yours Truly") and your name typed four lines below.

Place the cover letter on top of the résumé. Mail them together, flat, in a 9-inch (22 centimeter) by 12-inch (30 cm) envelope. Try to mail the envelope so that it gets to the agency on a Tuesday, Wednesday, or Thursday. Mondays are often hectic. Fridays are days employers want to wrap up and get away for the weekend. Mail that arrives in the middle of the week gets more attention. Some employers prefer that applicants apply online. An e-mail with the résumé sent as an attachment should look just like a hard-copy business letter. Avoid the casual language of most e-mail messages sent to friends and family.

Completing the Package

The next thing for an employment package is a list of references. Professional references are people who can talk about your qualifications. They can be past bosses, coworkers, clients, or people you have worked with in such volunteer activities as leading church or sports groups. Network contacts who know you well—especially those who work in the criminal justice field—would make good professional references.

Personal references are also known as character references. They talk about you as a person. Look for personal references among neighbors and friends. Teachers, coaches, and leaders of groups you've belonged to are good choices. They must know you well enough to talk about your personal traits and strengths. Avoid using family members.

Get permission from everyone before using his or her name as a reference. Ask in person or by telephone, letter, or e-mail. Tell each one about the job you seek. You can also list the qualities that make you a good candidate for it. Never "coach" the person about what to say.

Verify all addresses and phone numbers. Ask how they prefer to be contacted. Also ask if certain numbers are best called during specific times of the day. After a person agrees to provide a reference, send a personal, handwritten thank-you note.

Former teachers and leaders of organizations you have belonged to make good choices for personal references. They can talk about your character traits and skills. Ask permission to list them in your employment package.

Write the list. Include the person's name, job title, company, and contact information.

Finally, make copies of such documents as a high school diploma, first-aid or CPR certificate, and proof that you have had diversity or other special training. Put everything but the list of references in a businesslike folder to make it easy for the people you meet to handle. Provide the list of references only when asked.

CHAPTER FIVE

Talk to Me

A personal interview is the key to getting a job. It lets employers meet you and see how well you fit their agency. It's also a way to show you whether the agency is a place you want to work. A personal interview is a two-way process. Both parties exchange information.

For criminal justice jobs, the first interview is just that: a beginning. There will be more times to meet and talk with others during the hiring process. For example, there may be a psychological examination or polygraph test.

The first interview may be over the phone or in person. Later ones may be with different individuals or groups. All

A job interview is a chance to sell yourself and your skills and experience to an employer. It's also a chance for you to see if this is the best job or employer for you.

employer contacts affect the hiring decision. Some agencies ask candidates to appear before an oral board. An oral board is a meeting with several interviewers. They may all be professionals. Or some may be community members. Oral boards are most common for jobs in law enforcement and corrections. They may also be used for officers seeking promotions.

TYPICAL ORAL BOARD QUESTIONS

Oral boards are used to evaluate job applicants for law enforcement and corrections. Interviewers evaluate applicants on the ability to use good judgment and think under stress. The best answers are brief, specific, and truthful. Here are some sample questions for a job in juvenile corrections:

1. Your group of wards follows a daily schedule. Describe a situation when you supervised a large group of individuals. How did you ensure that everyone completed tasks correctly and on time?
2. One of a number of wards in a group you are supervising is using hostile language toward you and the other wards. How would you maintain control and keep other members of the group from joining in the same behavior?
3. Another corrections officer is using abusive language with a ward who had cursed at her. The situation is getting worse. What steps would you take?
4. Corrections officers often use intervention techniques to try to avoid physical intervention. Describe a time when you were able to prevent a situation from becoming physical.
5. What is a correction officer's role in keeping illegal drugs out of the facility?

Check Out the Employer

Before the interview, learn all you can about the agency and community where you will work. Visit the agency's Web site. Know its regulations and policies. How many employees are there? In a corrections setting, how many inmates are there? Is it a juvenile detention center or a maximum-security prison? Look for newspaper or magazine articles about the agency. The best place to search is a library's online databases.

For all jobs, including security ones, look for a local visitor's bureau for the city, county, and state. What is the population? What is the area's ethnic breakdown? How well

During the job application process, you'll get a look at the work environment. This maximum-security facility at the Arizona State Prison is an example of a place a corrections officer might work.

educated is the typical resident? What are the geographical boundaries of the city and county?

What to Wear

Dress for success. For formal interviews, the best choice is business clothes. Men should wear a sport coat and tie. Women need a business suit or conservative dress and closed-toed shoes. Post earrings are OK, but dangling earrings and gaudy jewelry aren't.

Always wear proper attire for any contact with the agency. If you're dropping off a copy of the reference list, for example, wear at least business-casual clothes. For men that means nice pants and a collared shirt; for women, pants with a suitable blouse are a good choice. Don't stop in wearing jeans and a T-shirt if you want every impression you make to be a good one. The receptionist may be a "secret" interviewer. In fact, some employers ask receptionists about a candidate's attitude and behavior during the wait for the actual interview.

Personal grooming is also important. Everything about your appearance says something about you. Get a haircut. Cover tattoos with long sleeves. Be sure to clean fingernails. And shine shoes. Men need neat facial hair—or a clean shave.

Arrive on Time

Never run in five minutes late, out of breath, with hair flying, and carrying loose papers. Arrive between ten and fifteen minutes early. Later shows lack of planning. Earlier makes you seem desperate for the job.

BODY LANGUAGE

Body language communicates without words. It includes posture, gestures, and facial expressions. Be aware of what your body language says about you.

- Posture: Sit and stand straight. Keep your back off the back of the chair. Lean a bit forward. Slouching says you don't care about what you're doing.
- Eye contact: Keep your gaze on the interviewer's eyes. During an oral board, look at the person who asks the question. As you answer, make eye contact with all members of the board. Eye contact shows interest. It also shows confidence and honesty.
- Leg and arm position: Keep arms to the side. When seated, keep knees together with feet flat on the floor. Crossed arms and legs say you don't like a person or that you disagree with him or her.
- Gestures: Use them. But don't use too many. Gestures emphasize particular points. They indicate comfort in the situation. However, constantly busy hands show nervousness. They distract from what you say.
- Fidgeting: Wiggling the body, scuffling feet, and playing with hair or jewelry indicate nervousness. Control your body to show confidence.

Days before the interview, practice getting to the agency at the same time of day as the interview. Compare different routes. Look for road construction that might cause delays. And pay attention to heavy traffic during rush hours between 6 AM and 9 AM and between 4 PM and 7 PM. If using public transportation, get the schedule. Ride the bus or train you will take to see how long the trip is.

A smile is the best accessory for a business suit at a job interview. Pay attention to proper grooming, and leave flashy jewelry at home.

Know exactly where to go. Which building and entrance should be used? How do you get to the interview room? Know where elevators and stairs are. Find the nearest rest-room for a last-minute check in the mirror. Try out the directions in the building before the interview day.

Practice

Being a little nervous before a job interview is normal. But don't let nerves give the impression that you lack confidence. One way to be more comfortable is to practice beforehand. Networking comes in handy here. Those chats are like job interviews.

List the kinds of questions the employer is likely to ask:

- Why do you want this type of job?
- Why do you want to work at this agency?
- What subjects did you like best in school?
- How can you contribute to this agency?
- What skills do you have that best suit you for the job?
- What areas would you like to improve?

Be ready with answers. Keep them brief, simple, and spe-cific. Ask a friend or family member to practice interviewing you. But don't memorize or rehearse too much. Your conver-sation should be easy and natural.

Turn off your cell phone before entering the room.

During the Interview

Expect to stay about a half hour for the interview. Stay calm. Start in a friendly, confident way. Be careful not to seem cocky.

Smile and use a firm handshake. If there is more than one interviewer, shake hands with each one. Use "Sir" or "Ma'am" to address them.

For a one-on-one interview, work on building a bond. If you notice a picture of the person fishing and you also like to fish, mention that. Ask about the person's favorite fishing spot, target fish, or bait. But stay respectful, not chummy. Let the interviewer take charge.

Carefully listen to questions. Speak slowly and clearly—and loud enough to be easily heard. Avoid slang expressions and inappropriate language. Answer the questions asked. Use specific examples to showcase your skills and experience. Don't exaggerate, veer away from the topic, or explain too much. Resist the urge to bad-mouth former employers or their companies. And, of course, tell the truth.

Ask questions of your own. Show that you're interested in the job. What duties would you perform during the probationary period? How many officers are on each shift? Ask the interviewer to clarify an answer. (The more you let him or her talk, the more he or she will like you.) Avoid questions about vacations or benefits. Focus on what you can do for the agency.

Take a cue from the interviewer about when to stop. Thank him or her. Shake hands. Send a handwritten thank-you note to each person you meet. When the time for a decision is near, call the contact person to follow up on your application. If you don't get the job, do another self-evaluation. Do you have the skills and other qualifications to be competitive? If not, get them. In the meantime, apply elsewhere.

CHAPTER SIX

The First Day and Beyond

You got the job! Now what do you do? Most new hires feel completely useless on the first day of work. You're not likely to go on a stakeout, walk a beat, or supervise inmate haircuts the first day. Instead, expect to be tied up in red tape and meetings with supervisors and coworkers.

The first stop is the human resources department. There is paperwork to fill out for federal and state withholding taxes, life and health insurance, and retirement benefits. There may be other information about new employee responsibilities, general information, resources, and policies.

You'll meet supervisors and coworkers. Greet each one with a smile and a firm handshake. Keep language and behavior friendly and professional. You may be assigned a training officer. If not, look for a mentor—someone who can guide your early career. A mentor shares information and knowledge gained through experience. He or she is someone who can help you grow personally and professionally. A mentor should be someone with whom you feel comfortable. A mentor may seek you out. Or you may approach him or her. Wait until you've had a chance to observe more experienced employees in action and decide who you'd like to work with.

Those who work in criminal justice careers must keep their finances in order. A bad credit rating can make you seem at risk for corruption. Follow a budget, save money, and pay bills on time.

Criminal justice jobs often require a good credit rating. Create a budget and live by it. Establish a savings account to use as an emergency fund. Add to it until you have two or three month's worth of take-home pay. Use credit cards wisely, and pay them on time. You need to avoid the appearance that you are in a position to be tempted by bribery, theft, or corruption.

Academies

Jobs in law enforcement and corrections often require academy training. Most agencies send new hires to a particular academy and pay for the training. Academies may be local, regional, state, or private. Some are commuter institutions. Students go home after each day's training. Others are residential, and students live at the academy during training.

Academies for law enforcement and corrections have both classroom instruction as well as training and supervised experience. For example, a police academy may hold classes in constitutional and state law, civil rights, and ethics. Practical training may include traffic control, self-defense, firearm use, first aid, and emergency response. When police officers graduate from the academy, they usually serve a probationary period. During that time, they get supervised on-the-job training.

Some corrections jobs require training instead of or in addition to formal academy instruction. Many offer training based on guidelines established by the American Correctional Association (ACA). Some state and local agencies provide supervised on-the-job training. Classes may include legal restrictions, interpersonal relations, self-defense, and use of firearms.

Security Licensure

Most states require licenses for security guards. Licenses may

Every morning, police recruits at the Chicago Police Academy attend a flag-raising ceremony honoring officers who have lost their lives in the line of duty.

differ for armed and unarmed guards. Work in casino surveillance may require additional training.

In some states, applicants attend state-certified training. They also undergo fingerprinting and background checks. Security job seekers may also want or need certification for protection professionals in addition to licensure. ASIS International offers such certification. It also provides voluntary guidelines and training that may be necessary in some states.

Examples of ASIS training include:

- Protection
- Public relations
- Report writing
- First aid
- Deterring crises
- Special training for particular assignments

To find what licenses and certification are needed or preferred, ask your employer or call the types of security employers where you'd like to work. They will help you enroll for the coursework and testing processes.

The Annual or Probation Review

At the end of the probationary period, or at the end of a year on the job, there will likely be a review of your performance. This review is similar to a job interview. This time, though, the employer has your specific performance to discuss.

During the review, list your accomplishments during the review period. Mention new things you have learned on the job. Add any additional training or college courses you have taken. Also, be ready to discuss mistakes and areas that you or the employer thinks you can improve. Talk about specific steps you have taken to remedy errors or prevent making a similar mistake in the future. During the meeting, listen respectfully. Control your emotions. Don't argue and don't complain. Look for an opportunity to discuss your short-term and long-term career goals. Ask what the supervisor recommends you do to achieve them.

Getting Ahead

The key to getting ahead in criminal justice jobs is continuing education. Some agencies pay tuition or offer other incentives for college classes, conferences, or other special training. Even if they don't, it may be worth it to enroll and pay for them yourself.

Many law enforcement and corrections jobs fall under the heading of civil service. Civil service workers are non-political government employees outside judicial, legislative, or military services. They are usually hired and promoted on the basis of competitive examinations. The tests may be held on a specific schedule or as needed to fill openings. The tests are open to anyone who has the qualifications for the job. Get information about the appropriate exams from your supervisor or human resources department. Also ask where to find study guides and sample tests. Employers in the private sector sometimes use written tests to screen job applicants. If you are asked to take such a test, ask how best to prepare for it.

College classes, conferences, and other special training are keys to advance in a criminal justice career. Lifelong learning should continue after you land a job.

Preparing for Promotional Tests

A professional approach to written tests increases the chances of success. Find out what kind of test it will be. Is it a general knowledge test or a test of job-specific knowledge? If a test covers math, reading, grammar, and writing, study each separately. Start with your weakest subject. The Internet is your best friend. Simply search for the topic and "test preparation." Take some online practice exams. Many are free. For job-specific exams, ask the employer or testing facility where to find sample questions and practice them.

Use the same strategies you use for a job interview. Before the test day, take a trial run to the testing center. Make note of the best route and travel time. Get plenty of sleep the night before. Eat a light, balanced breakfast. Limit the amount of caffeine. Arrive ten to fifteen minutes early. Wear comfortable, professional clothing and a working wristwatch. You'll want to keep track of how much time you have left during the exam. Stay mentally positive before and during the test. Negative thoughts can drag you down and hurt your results.

Bring two No. 2 pencils and a signed photo ID to the test site. Do not bring any written materials (other than an admission notice). Leave cell phones, beepers, headphones, and other electronic devices at home or in the car.

Test-taking Tips

Pay close attention to the verbal and written instructions. If there's something you don't understand, ask the test supervisor to clarify it.

Be clear about time limits. Some tests must be completed within a certain total time period. Other tests are timed according to each separate section. Divide the time you have by the number of questions. This will give you a good idea of how much time to spend on each one. Keep moving through the test at a steady pace. Don't spend too much time on any one question. Give the best answer you can, and move on. Trust your knowledge and experience.

Answer all of the questions. And answer each question in order. If you skip around, you might forget to go back to some questions. Or you could get confused about where to put answers on the answer sheet.

Carefully read each question. Watch for words that affect meaning. Examples are negatives words like "not," "except," "never," and "least." Also watch for such words as "probably," "may," "might," and "sometimes." But try not to read too much into a question. The simplest interpretation and most logical answer are usually correct.

If you finish early, go back and check your work. Reread questions to be sure you understood them the first time. However, try not to second-guess yourself. The first answer you think of is usually correct.

Good luck! The road to a career in law enforcement can be a difficult one, but one that is very rewarding.

agility The ability to move quickly and gracefully.

civil service employee A government employee outside judicial, legislative, or military services.

cover letter An individually typed letter that "covers" a résumé in an envelope.

elevator speech A speech a person could give if he or she could talk only for the length of an elevator ride with someone.

endurance The ability to do an activity for a long period of time.

General Equivalency Degree (GED) test A written test that measures the main ideas and skills associated with four years of high school classes.

in-service training Employee education provided by the employer aimed at developing or improving skills.

jurisdiction The area where a police officer or other government official has authority.

mentor An experienced person in a profession who shares information and knowledge gained and guides a new hire's early career, as well as personal and professional growth.

networking Using a group of friends and other contacts to learn information or share services.

oral board A meeting with a group of several interviewers to evaluate a candidate for a criminal justice job.

orienteering Using a map and compass to find one's way across an unknown area. A race may be held based on this skill.

personal reference A person an employer can contact to discuss an applicant's character traits.

polygraph A machine that measures changes in heartbeat, blood pressure, and respiration in an effort to tell whether a person is telling the truth.

professional reference A person an employer can contact to ask about an applicant's qualifications for a job.

résumé A list of a job seeker's education, experiences, skills, and interests.

trajectory The path of a moving body, such as a bullet, through space.

topographical map A map of an area that shows the position and height above sea level of such features as lakes, rivers, forests, roads, and buildings.

American Correctional Association
206 North Washington Street, Suite 200
Alexandria, VA 22314
(800) ACA-JOIN (222-5646)
Web site: http://aca.org
The American Correctional Association offers professional
development, certification, and accreditation to all members of the corrections profession. It also provides a job
bank for members.

ASIS International
1625 Prince Street
Alexandria, VA 22314-2818
(703) 519-6200
Web site: http://www.asisonline.org
Formerly known as the American Society for Industrial
Security, ASIS International is an organization of thirty-
eight thousand security professionals in two hundred
chapters worldwide. It develops educational and certification programs and materials.

Canadian Police Association
Suite 100
141 Catherine Street
Ottawa, ON K2P 1C3
Canada
(613) 231-4168
Web site: http://www.cpa-acp.ca
The Canadian Police Association is a national voice and
support network for police officers in Canada. It also

connects members with the international police community.

International Association of Women Police
P.O. Box 184
Marble Hill, GA 30148
Web site: http://www.iawp.oprg
Women police officers from sixty countries belong to this organization. Its mission is "to strengthen, unite, and raise the profile of women in criminal justice internationally."

National Association of Police Organizations (NAPO)
317 South Patrick Street
Alexandria, VA 22314-3501
(703) 549-0775
Web site: http://napo.org
NAPO is an organization of more than two thousand American police unions and associations. It uses legal advocacy, political action, and education to serve more than 241,000 sworn law enforcement officers and other members.

National Association of School Resource Officers (NASRO)
2020 Valleydale Road, Suite 207A
Hoover, AL 35244
(888) 316-2776
Web site: http://www.nasro.org
NASRO is a nonprofit organization for school-based law enforcement officers, school administrators, and school security and safety professionals. It offers

training, networking opportunities, and support for its members.

National Black Police Association
3100 Main Street #256
Dallas, TX 75226
(855) 879-6272
Web site: http://blackpolice.org
This nonprofit organization works to improve the interactions between police departments and minority communities. It also helps recruit minority police officers nationwide and works to eliminate police corruption, brutality, and racial discrimination.

National Coalition of Community-Based Correctional and Community Re-entry Organizations (NC4RSO)
250 H Street #224
Blaine, WA 98230
(360) 752-4452
Web site: http://www.nc4rso.org
NC4RSO is nonprofit group of community organizations that offer programs in jails, prisons, and community re-entry throughout the United States.

National Institute of Corrections (NIC)
320 First Street NW
Washington, DC 20543
(800) 995-6423
Web site: http://www.nicic.org
NIC is a federal agency that is part of the U.S. Department of Justice, Federal Bureau of Prisons. It provides training,

technical assistance, information services, and policy and program development assistance to federal, state, and local corrections agencies.

National Partnership for Juvenile Services
2220 Nicholasville Road, Suite 110–333
Lexington, KY 40503
(859) 333-2584
Web site: http://npjs.org
In 2004, members of the Council for Educators of At-Risk and Delinquent Youth, the Juvenile Justice Trainers Association, the National Association for Juvenile Correctional Agencies, and the National Juvenile Detention Association merged under one structure. Services include professional development and a job bank.

Royal Canadian Mounted Police
CMP National Headquarters
Headquarters Building
73 Leikin Drive
Ottawa, ON K1A 0R2
Canada
(613) 993-7267
Web site: http://www.rcmp-grc.gc.ca
The Royal Canadian Mounted Police is Canada's national police service. It serves federal bodies, as well as provinces, cities, territories, aboriginal communities, and three international airports.

World Association of Detectives
7501 Sparrows Point Boulevard

Baltimore, MD 21219 USA
(443) 982-4586
Web site: http://wad.net
Formed as a joint venture of the combined membership of the World Association of Detectives and the International Secret Service Association, this organization promotes ethical practices for private investigators and security service personnel.

Web Sites

Due to the changing nature of Internet links, Rosen Publishing has developed an online list of Web sites related to the subject of this book. This site is updated regularly. Please use this link to access the list:

http://www.rosenlinks.com/JOBS/Law

Bagley, Paul D. *The Everything Guide to Careers in Law Enforcement.* Avon, MA: FW Media, 2011.

Blackwell, Amy Hackney. *Law Enforcement and Public Safety.* New York, NY: Ferguson Publishing, 2011.

Brezina, Corona. *Careers in Law Enforcement.* New York, NY: Rosen Classroom, 2009.

Chertavian, Gerald. *A Year Up: How a Pioneering Program Teaches Young Adults Real Skills for Real Jobs—With Real Success.* New York, NY: Viking Adult, 2012.

Dixon, Steve. *Police Stories: Making One Bit of Difference.* Morgan Hill, CA: Tonawanda Press, 2011.

Duffin, Allan T. *History in Blue: 160 Years of Women Police, Sheriffs, Detectives, and State Troopers.* New York, NY: Kaplan Publishing, 2010.

Edge, Laura B. *Locked Up: A History of the U.S. Prison System.* Minneapolis, MN: 21st Century, 2009.

Ferguson Publishing. *Ferguson's Careers in Focus: Public Safety.* New York, NY: Ferguson Publishing, 2007.

Fry, Ron. *101 Smart Questions to Ask on Your Interview.* Pompton Plains, NJ: Career Press, 2012.

Learning Express editors. *Becoming a Homeland Security Professional.* New York, NY: Learning Express, 2010.

Molidor, John B. *Crazy Good Interviewing: How Acting a Little Crazy Can Get You the Job.* Hoboken, NJ: Wiley 2012.

Rorhus, Suzanne, and Bill Howe. *Cuffed: Armed with Words and Armed and Trained.* Orlando, FL: Echelon Press, 2012.

Saddleback Educational Publishing. *Workplace and Career Words.* Costa Mesa, CA: Saddleback Educational Publishing, 2011.

Schuman, Nancy. *1,001 Phrases You Need to Get a Job.* Avon, MA: Adams Media, 2012.

Snow, Robert L. *Policewomen Who Made History: Breaking Through the Ranks.* Lanham, MD: Rowman and Littlefield, 2010.

Spell, David. *Street Cop.* Eugene, OR: Resource Publications, 2010.

Timony, John F. *Beat Cop to Top Cop.* Philadelphia, PA: University of Pennsylvania Press, 2010.

Watson, Stephanie. *A Career as a Police Officer.* New York, NY: Rosen Classroom, 2010.

Williamson, Carolyn. *Ultimate Interview: 100s of Great Interview Answers.* Philadelphia, PA: Kogan Page, 2008.

Bureau of Labor Statistics, U.S. Department of Labor. "Correctional Officers." *Occupational Outlook Handbook, 2012–13*, April 26, 2012. Retrieved May 27, 2012 (http://www.bls.gov/ooh/protective-service/correctional-officers.htm).

Bureau of Labor Statistics, U.S. Department of Labor. "Police and Detectives." *Occupational Outlook Handbook, 2012–13*, April 26, 2012. Retrieved May 27, 2012 (http://www.bls.gov/ooh/protective-service/correctional-officers.htm).

Bureau of Labor Statistics, U.S. Department of Labor. "Security Guards and Gaming Surveillance Officers." *Occupational Outlook Handbook, 2012–13*, March 29, 2012. Retrieved May 27, 2012 (http://www.bls.gov/ooh/protective-service/correctional-officers.htm).

Douglas, John. *John Douglas's Guide to the Police Officer Exams.* New York, NY: Kaplan Publishing, 2011.

Duffin, Allan T. *History in Blue: 1604 Years of Women Police, Sheriffs, Detectives, and State Troopers.* New York, NY: Kaplan Publishing, 2010.

Grant, Heath B., and Karen J. Terry. *Law Enforcement in the 21st Century.* Boston, MA: Pearson, 2012.

Harr, J. Scott, and Karen M. Hess. *Careers in Criminal Justice and Related Fields: From Internship to Promotion.* Belmont, CA: Wadsworth Cengage Learning, 2010.

LearningExpress. *Becoming a Police Officer.* New York, NY: Learning Express, 2009.

Martin, Carole. "Top Ten Tips to Boost Your Interview IQ." Monster.com, March 20, 2009. Retrieved June 9, 2012 (http://www.fastweb.com/career-planning/articles/323-top-ten-tips-to-boost-your-interview-iq).

Petryszyn, Kelly. "Number of Women Police Officers Rising."
    Morning Journal, February 12, 2012. Retrieved June 21,
    2012 (http://www.morningjournal.com/articles/2012/02
    /12/news/mj5720378.txt?viewmode=fullstory).
Potter, Caroline M. "Seven Job Search Mistakes New Grads
    Make." Monster.com, 2012. Retrieved May 25, 2012
    (http://career-advice.monster.com/job-search/getting-
    started/7-jobsearch-mistakes-new-grads-make-hot-jobs
    /article.aspx).
TipTopJob.com. "Top Ten Interview Tips." TipTopJob.com,
    2012. Retrieved June 9, 2012 (http://tiptopjob.com
    /displaycontent/sectionid/15/contentid/701_top
    _ten_interview_tips).
U.S. Census Bureau. "Profile America Facts for Features."
    January 26, 2011. Retrieved June 21, 2012 (http://www
    .census.gov/newsroom/releases/archives/facts_for
    _features_special_editions/cb11-ff04.html).
Wynn, Michael. *Rising Through the Ranks: Leadership Tools and
    Techniques for Law Enforcement*. New York, NY: Kaplan
    Publishing.

About the Author

Mary-Lane Kamberg is a professional writer and speaker who specializes in nonfiction for children and adults. She has published twenty-two books, including fourteen for young readers. She once served as a police matron for a municipal police department.

Photo Credits

Cover, p. 1 © iStockphoto.com/sjlocke; cover (background), back cover © iStockphoto.com/Anton Prado Photography; p. 3, interior page background image Pete Ryan/National Geographic/Getty Images; p. 5 Ron Phillips/© Warner Bros./ courtesy Everett Collection; pp. 8–9 bikeriderlondon/ Shutterstock.com; pp. 10–11, 19, 49, 62–63 © AP Images: p. 14 Creatas Images/Thinkstock; p. 22 samotrebizan/Shutterstock. com; pp. 26–27 Commercial Eye/Iconica/Getty Images; p. 29 © iStockphoto.com./Alex Gumerov: p. 33 Yellow Dog Productions/The Image Bank/Getty Images; p. 35 © iStockphoto.com/Anatoly Vartanov: p. 39 Monkey Business Images/Shutterstock.com: pp. 44–45 Keith Brofsky/UpperCut Images/Getty Images; pp. 46–47 © iStockphoto.com/Steve Debenport; p. 52 Comstock Images/Getty Images; pp. 56–57 iStockphoto/Thinkstock; pp. 58–59 Scott Olson/Getty Images.

Designer: Brian Garvey; Editor: Bethany Bryan; Photo Researcher: Marty Levick